P RAY
with me
S TILL

P RAY
with me
S TILL

*Rosary Meditations and Spiritual Support
for Persons with Alzheimer's,
Their Caregivers, and Loved Ones*

Holy Cross Family Ministries

ave maria press AmP Notre Dame, Indiana

www.avemariapress.com

ISBN-10 1-59471-077-5
ISBN-13 978-1-59471-077-3

Cover and text design by Brian C. Conley

Printed and bound in the United States of America.

Library of Congress Cataloging-in-Publication Data
Pray with me still : rosary meditations and spiritual support for persons with Alzheimer's, their caregivers, and loved ones / Holy Cross Family Ministries.
   p. cm.
  ISBN-13: 978-1-59471-077-3 (pbk.)
  ISBN-10: 1-59471-077-5 (pbk.)
  1. Alzheimer's disease—Patients—Religious life. 2. Alzheimer's disease—Religious aspects—Catholic Church. 3. Alzheimer's disease—Prayer-books and devotions—Engish. 4. Rosary. I. Holy Cross Family Ministries.

  BV4910.6.A55P73 2006
  242'.4—dc22
                                       2005031892

Contents

Foreword

This book offers spiritual support meditations on the Mysteries of the Rosary directly related to the experience of those many people who accompany a loved one with Alzheimer's disease or another form of dementia. Prayer is one of the few ways of coping with such a reality. Prayer, as it turns out, also remains a vibrant part of the life of one who suffers with the disease.

When my mother died, all of her grown children knew it would be a most difficult blow for our father. It turned out that Dad was unable to process the reality of her death, or even the fact that he had attended both the wake and the funeral. There was anger and confusion over the accusation he made: "You never told me about this!" Mom had been shielding us from the reality that Dad was not picking up on everything. For quite some time, we would ask him a question and Mom answered. It was a pattern we'd seen before; nothing unusual for a couple who had been married for so many years. We hadn't realized that Dad's world was becoming so limited. We just didn't recognize it.

After our mother's death, we began to witness Dad's slow submission to Alzheimer's disease. He stayed for five years in the apartment he had shared with my mom, but one of my sisters actually made his meals most nights and frequently stayed the night so he would not be so confused and lonely. He kept his car but did not take it anywhere for years since he was not sure of the way back. Luckily, he was never one to cook anything, or he would surely have left the oven or stove burners on. We hired people to stay with him during the day, since we were afraid he would wander off and not find his way home. He accepted that most days, but then one day he would say: "You are following me around all the time. You're fired!"

When we took Dad to a nursing home, he was angry with everyone, but especially with me. He knew I had some kind of deciding vote in this regard. He wore an ankle bracelet that would set off an alarm if he went outside. He missed the ease of home, but eventually reconciled with the fact that he needed the kind of help given there. Dad was more upbeat than most residents were, so the sisters would take him around to help cheer up the other residents. He often used his considerable social skills to hide the fact that he had no clue who people were. The four years Dad spent at St. Patrick's Nursing Home in Framingham, Massachusetts, under the care of the Carmelite Sisters of the Aged and Infirmed, confirmed us all in the knowledge that he was safe and needed to be there. But there were heartbreaks as well. He would go through every emotion and so would we.

A few of us attended seminars in which we learned about the disorientation caused later in the day by "sundowning" and the confusion caused by mirrors for someone with Alzheimer's. Dad even tried to pick a fight once with a cocky guy glaring at him from a mirror. Luckily, no punches were thrown. On the positive side, my dad, a former bandleader, loved to visit the "pub" in the nursing home, where residents and volunteers sang the songs of their youth, which never grew old for them.

The great tendency for families when they reach the stage where their loved one is no longer able to recognize them is to believe that the person is now beyond reach because he or she cannot identify others. But this is untrue and too hasty a conclusion. To the day of his death, my father never lost his faith, his sense of humor, or his love for music, though he lost much else.

This Rosary book can perhaps remind us how those stricken with Alzheimer's are still people of faith. Even though my dad may have been nine years old again in his mind, that was an age in which he knew there was a God and prayed the Rosary. Our message is: Keep praying with those who suffer from Alzheimer's. Even if they do not know your name or remember all the words of the prayers, they do know God's name and they continue to experience an ever-growing need for God.

When Dad died, we were gathered around the bed. After praying the Rosary, we began singing the old songs he'd loved so well. We sang about dying: "Swing Low, Sweet Chariot," "Soon and Very Soon," "When the Saints Go Marching In." We like to think that the infinitely better heavenly choir singing "Glory to God" interrupted our singing and our tears. And we like to think that Dad, whom we have known in his severe limitation, chimed in right on key!

Read the meditations offered in this book with care. And pray through your experience these unique mysteries of the Rosary. God is never far from us and, as our founder, Servant of God Father Patrick Peyton, CSC, was so fond of saying, "The family that prays together stays together."

REV. JOHN PHALEN, CSC
PRESIDENT OF HOLY CROSS FAMILY MINISTRIES

Preface

This book combines the work, study, experience, and love of dedicated people who know and care for persons with Alzheimer's disease. Father John Malecki, a psychologist in the Albany Diocese, counsels and prays with persons with Alzheimer's disease. Maggie Hume cared for her mother at home with her husband and five children. Father John Phalen, CSC, lived through the difficult experience of his dad's Alzheimer's as he was cared for in a nursing home. I have ministered with the sick and the dying in parish ministry and offer some of my perspective on the spiritual dimensions of the disease. Our experiences are expressed in this book. Father Malecki contributes his research into the spiritual lives of Alzheimer's patients, Maggie Hume her meditations on the mysteries of the Rosary and how she lived those mysteries in the everyday care of her mother. Father Phalen shares with us his family's experience of accompanying their dad through the difficult phases of the disease. And I have written Rosary meditations for those with Alzheimer's and their loved ones and have gathered all of the pieces for this book.

We hope *Pray With Me Still* helps all of us be more attentive to the spiritual depth and needs of people living with Alzheimer's. We hope, too, that you who read it are encouraged knowing that the faith your loved one developed earlier in life remains an important source of strength at this time of struggle and fear. While some of you will read and digest this book from cover to cover, others will choose to sink right into praying with the Rosary meditations. Prayer can be a shared comfort between the person with the disease and his or her caregivers and loved ones. This book is meant to give hope and support to all.

BETH MAHONEY,
MISSION DIRECTOR
HOLY CROSS FAMILY MINISTRIES

1
—

The Spiritual Life and Alzheimer's Disease: Three Case Studies
by Fr. John Malecki

ANDREW

During a group session with Alzheimer's patients, Andrew became urgently sick. The nurses sent for an ambulance to transfer him to a nearby acute-care hospital. While waiting for the ambulance, I asked Andrew how we could help and support him. He looked around the room and said in a quiet, heartfelt tone, "I ask my friends to pray with me as I face this pain and fear." With virtually no time lapse, Carolyn replied, "Count on us to pray with you, because all of us need to ask for help and understanding—in or out of church."

These words triggered an equally spontaneous expression from Elizabeth, another group member, who said, "Of course we will pray with you, but then I pray all day long because I relate to God the way my body relates to gravity. It's always there—a constant relationship." She went on to describe how through prayer she became aware of what is in her—the positive and the negative, the best and the worst. In her words,

"Sometimes I fight with God, (no holds barred) and at other times, I have the picture of embracing God in love."

To some extent, Elizabeth's images reveal how primary-process thinking operates in all of us all the time. What the founder of psychoanalysis, Sigmund Freud, called primary-process thinking was termed fantasy thinking by successor and sometimes rival, psychologist Carl Jung. Essentially, this mentality is a primordial or foundational experience, an expression of instinctual activity. It is amoral, characterized by wishes, transcends time and space, and is ruled by the pleasure principle. Hence, primary-process or fantasy thinking usually dominates in infancy and childhood, as well as in creative moments of artistic expression, religious experience, and also in such pathological conditions as schizophrenia and autism. It is no surprise to find that there is a universal fear of this primary level of experience and interpretive thought. However, it is at this very level of thought experience that both Freud and Jung locate the function of religion within the human psyche.

Freud opposed religion, believing that religion is an illusion that does not provide a true means by which humans can interpret the most fundamental or primordial of experiences. Religion deludes people by providing rituals so that people can avoid dealing with the harshness of reality, encourages people to project wishes for satisfaction and safety onto a "divine Santa Claus" who rewards every time people promise to be good. In effect, religion keeps people in "psychological shortpants."

In sharp contrast, Jung acknowledged religion as a necessary aspect of human experience and insisted that it does provide an appropriate and necessary way for humans to interpret reality. In other words, religion provides a structure for fantasy or primary-process thinking.

Jung believed that directed and fantasy thinking coexist as two separate and equal perspectives or capacities in the human mind. His teaching is confirmed in current brain research, which describes the functioning of the two cerebral hemispheres, the interaction of which is essential to mental functioning. The left hemisphere is associated with language abilities, logic, aim-directed action and it obeys laws of time and space. These left hemisphere operations are often characterized as analytical and rational. In comparison, the right hemisphere is identified as the site of emotions, feelings, and fantasies, the capacity to recognize where one is in relation to everything else and a holistic grasp of complex situations.

While Jung's fantasy or primary-process thinking clearly belongs to the right hemisphere of the brain, Ann and Barry Ulanov contribute this imagery in portraying it further:

> Primary process may be likened to a rushing river of being—a tumult of unformulated strongly felt wishes, of partial images, affective impulses, pulsating instincts, insistent urges, and compelling drives. It is inexhaustible, an eternal flow of life in its most elemental form, coursing beneath all the modulated actions, rational intentions, and measured involvements with one another that we may erect above it (Ulanov, *Religion and the Unconscious*, p. 26).

This sphere of our psyche's functions leads us straight to the workings of our soul. Each time a person calls for help from forces beyond us, we pray to something that appears to answer us human beings. From a psychological point of view, we recognize:

> Prayer's first act of confession is the discovery of this primary speech. We begin to hear the self, we actually are emerging out of our shadow selves, our counterfeit selves, our pretended selves . . . in prayer we say who we are—not who we should be nor who we wish we were, but who we are (Ulanov, *Primary Speech: A Psychology of Prayer*, p.1–2).

This experience of prayer as primary speech is more fundamental and basic to the psyche than the abstractions of organized, institutional religion. Prayer in this sense is pre-verbal; it exists in us from the beginning, from the very moment of birth. Prayer occurs when the nursing infant discovers that the flow of milk from its mother's breasts is or is not accessible and plentiful. As Melanie Klein observed, the concepts of "good" and "bad" are formulated at that point (Klein, *Envy and Gratitude and Other Works*, p. 2). Prayer emerges in a similar way. We are brought to our knees by fear or a strong need to reach out to something or someone beyond ourselves that we sense is there. The image of a mother caring for her nursling is the way John of the Cross describes God's response to the beginner in prayer (*Dark Night of the Soul*, p. 330). Even before we utter our first words, distinctions of value take place, which get interpreted into motions of prayer. Thus, a spiritual world begins to develop. What is so amazing about primary speech is that a new human being communicates to us in three messages: first, that it is a new being; second, that it is here; third, that it is.

In light of the above considerations, we can better appreciate that when Andrew lost his ability to formulate words, his groans for help were prayer as primary speech. The spontaneous outpouring of Elizabeth was a cauldron containing both directed and fantasy thinking. The seemingly unrestrained manner of her expression evoked awe and some degree of fear in other group members, particularly, as she gave a vivid portrayal of her "fights" with God and then how she lovingly surrendered into the arms of the God within her.

DAVID

Prayer as primary speech provides a path to our interior reality whatever it may be, positive or negative. To deny that reality or block availability to it leads to the diminution of the person. Honest admission is crucial in the development of primary speech as prayer. The experience of another of the patients in our group dramatically illustrates this.

David was a clergyperson, quiet, dignified, refined, friendly, and pleasant. After the third session, he began to experience what some describe as "unwanted emotional outbursts" and disturbing reactions. In a raucous angry tone he expressed hostility toward nurses and aides, regaled some of the patients with colorful profanity, shocked others with his words of bitterness towards God about his memory losses, and felt plagued in his imagination by intrusive images of lewd dancing girls.

Fantasy thinking (primary-process) was at work. As he calmed down, and felt some degree of reflection on what poured out of him, I communicated what I might say to all people. It is critical to stop denying what is in us, whether it is self-serving ambition, demeaning hostility, or a lusty sexuality. There is a long-honored asceticism of institutional religion that urges people to fear and even deny such thinking and images as representing evil within us. Honestly acknowledging the claims of reality within us is essential to the growth of primary speech as prayer. These things exist in us. It is unhealthy to scold or exclude parts of ourselves.

Our proper cleric felt guilt and shame for experiencing that flood of dancing girl images. His prayer as primary speech would move forward in a healthy direction if he were to say, "Yes, I admit they are there. What a remarkable thing! I am still alive." That expression of prayer opens us to the recognition that "we speak out of our 'flesh,' the ground of all our experiences" (Ulanov, *Primary Speech: A Psychology of Prayer*, p.1). It is an opportunity to recognize that God, who became flesh, meets us fully in the experience of what it means to be a human being. As primary speech unfolds in prayer, it is important to acknowledge that the spirit dwells in our flesh—being at last comes to be first.

EDITH

I noticed the absence of Edith, an eighty-three-year-old Alzheimer's patient, at our second group meeting. I went in search of her and found her in a bay window area of the dining room. Her brow was furrowed in anger, and her eyes had a lost, vacant look. I sat beside her and asked, "Could we talk?" She replied in a tone, which was a mixture of fear and anger, "What am I doing in this place? How do I get out of here?" Her questions poured out of her without any expectation of an answer, and continued with images of fantasy thinking and elements of conscious awareness of her here and now presence in the nursing home.

"I want to go back to Syracuse," she continued, "to be with the second grade school children I taught. I feel lonely without them. Their bright smiling faces gave me the feeling of Christ present in my heart—and I have lost that feeling. I am asking for help and understanding." I replied in the form of an ancient Slavic parable.

Once there was a little girl who lived with her parents in a fine house. It was customary for the parents to pray with their daughter at night and then put her to bed. It so happened that she awakened in the middle of the night. The angel of the Lord appeared to her and asked, "Are you alone in the house?" and she answered "No." The angel asked again, "If you wake up in the dark at night, would you know if your parents went on a journey?" and she answered, "Yes." The angel persisted in further questioning, "How would you know that you were not alone in the house? Would you see them and look at them?" the girl said, "No." The angel said, "Would you hear them? Is that how you'd know?" The girl said "No." The angel said, "Would they talk to you? Is that how you would know them?" Again the girl said, "No." And she thought to herself that this angel is asking stupid questions like a grown up. Finally the girl said to the angel with sureness of a wise old mother. "I would just know—I would just know that I wasn't alone in the house."

Change came over Edith's face. She relaxed and her face brightened as she said simply, "I just know." I am reminded that when Jung was asked if he believed in God, he answered, "I know. I don't need to believe. I know."

It is of central importance that with all the other images, images of God be brought into our prayer. These images may come from our worship, culture, or wherever we locate our faith. Some of the AD patients found images of God in the Bible—the good shepherd, the true vine, or the hand of God. Still others found images of God in nature, such as the evergreen tree. There are some who may find the images of God as characterized by their lack—an empty grayness, an absence. The fear here is that nothing will greet us from beyond—that there will be no image of God at all.

Perhaps, when our prayer is primary speech, we do not change what is outside ourselves; rather we change what is inside us. In prayer we do not change life but rather we transform our experiences of life. We narrow the gap between our unconscious and our consciousness, because there is change in both. We move from the futile efforts of the isolated ego trying to make things happen, to a greater reality—the Self, the unknown. I think that Alzheimer's patients often reach a level in their prayer experience where they relinquish their frantic efforts to control life, and make the surrender to belong to life. In their primary speech as prayer, they recognize that we are moved and that there is that which moves us—the Self, the rushing river of being. May we meet them there, love, and learn from them.

2
—

Our Spiritual Journey
by Beth Mahoney

The scripture passage from Psalm 130 that reads "Out of the depths I cry to you O Lord" has much meaning for those suffering from Alzheimer's disease and it can also be true for those caring for a sick loved one. How often do we feel that God is not with us or that we have turned from God because we do not understand the situation that we are faced with in life? This is true when we experience a loved one suffering from dementia. From deep within we call out to God for help.

It is a painful and difficult time when a loved one begins to lose their ability to respond to questions or interact in conversation that used to be enjoyable and stimulating for both of you. However, we can keep in mind that this person is a child of God and is a loving human being who has given us much life and love—often through a lifetime. When we can do that, we begin to see the beauty that is within him or her even if we can no longer relate to our loved one as we once did.

Scripture can bring us comfort and consolation in the midst of our struggles. It helps us relate to our loved ones who have entered into a new world all their own and who can no longer recognize us for who we are in their lives. It is truly a struggle to understand how these relationships have changed. We need to look not so much at the mother or father or other loved one who can no longer respond in the manner to which we are accustomed, but at our way of thinking and acting in our relationship with that person. It is our responsibility to look at her as who she is now, to respond to him in the here and now and not to lose sight of the person he is at this moment, in this place.

The Alzheimer's patient will often communicate in the prayer of primary speech that Fr. Malecki describes. Many seemingly nonsensical words may tumble out. The challenge is for the family member, friend, or caregiver to "Listen to my Soul!" as one frustrated patient instructed Fr. Malecki. Listen to her soul, indeed. Comprehend beyond the significance of the words themselves. Know that a fellow human being is frightened by the loss of faculties and the ability to communicate clearly and is reverting to primary speech to express his or her reality, much as a baby may speak gibberish with an intonation that implies "This makes sense!" We are told by Jesus to become as little children. Can we listen deeply to the child still dwelling in our loved one's soul?

The Spirit of God is alive and well within Alzheimer's patients as within us all and it needs to be nurtured. We need to greet the Spirit when we greet our loved one who is ill. Praying the Rosary and meditating on the scripture stories upon which it is built is one way for us to reconnect or remain connected to our loved one who is suffering from dementia. This book offers meditations on the mysteries of the Rosary to assist us in praying and reflecting on what we are living in our lives at the moment. The mysteries of the Rosary are indeed the mysteries of our own lives. Our moments of joy, sorrow, and glory, and of reconciliation and forgiveness, are brought into clearer focus in prayer. For example, we all can recall a time in our lives when we were called to do something like Mary in the Annunciation, saying "Yes" to something unknown and frightening. We've also had moments when we assist others in life to carry their burdens as Jesus did in the Carrying of the Cross.

Scripture can be a wonderful tool in helping us with praying the Rosary and reflecting on whatever we are faced with in life. In the Old Testament, we hear from the prophets Isaiah and Jeremiah, who reveal for us that God is with us. Isaiah tells us that God has grasped us by the hand, formed us, and set us to proclaim justice to all peoples (Is 42). Jeremiah reminds us that we can trust in God and that we can hand over our problems and concerns to God who hears us (Jer 20). How true this is for those who live with Alzheimer's disease, either as patients or as caregivers! So very often we need to be reminded that God is with us, that God will hear our prayers, and answer them. And that we can rest in God's peace and undying love.

Scripture can bring each one of us some strength, comfort, and consolation that we are relating, communicating, and praying with our loved one, even if there is no response or the response does not make sense to us. The words in Psalm 130 ring out from deep within each one of us and keep us connected to each other and to God:

"Out of the depths I cry to you O Lord!"

Other scripture passages to use when praying the Rosary:

Matthew 6:5–15	All the Mysteries
Luke 1:46–55	Joyful Mysteries
Mark 14:32–42	Sorrowful Mysteries
John 15:1–17	Luminous Mysteries
Isaiah 42:1–9	All the Mysteries—especially the Joyful Mysteries
Jeremiah 20:7–18	Sorrowful Mysteries
Psalm 23	All the Mysteries
Psalm 61	Glorious Mysteries
Psalm 95	All the Mysteries—especially the Joyful Mysteries
Psalm 123	Glorious Mysteries
Psalm 31	All the Mysteries—especially the Luminous Mysteries
Psalm 19	All the Mysteries—especially the Luminous Mysteries
Psalm 22	Sorrowful Mysteries
Psalm 25	Glorious Mysteries

3

How to Pray the Rosary

The Rosary is a prayer of meditation. We use the beads to focus our attention on the life of Christ through the Joyful, Luminous, Sorrowful, and Glorious Mysteries.

Praying in this way helps us to link our lives with what we know of the life of Jesus, Mary, and Joseph. It is one way God can show us that there is no part of our joy, pain, or glory where He is not present. There are two common ways to pray the Rosary in use today. One gathers all the prayers together to be said at once. This can be done alone or with a group (as in a family Rosary). The second method allows us to take a whole day to pray.

METHOD ONE
1. Looking at the cross, we hold it while we make the sign of the cross and pray the Apostles' Creed which is a summary of all the things we believe.
2. On this first large bead, we pray an Our Father, the prayer that Jesus taught us.
3. On each of the three smaller beads, we pray the Hail Mary. Then we pray the Glory Be.
4. On the next large bead, we announce the first mystery (of Joy, Light, Sorrow, or Glory). We reflect on what happened to Jesus at this time

and we think about what it means in our lives today. (At this point, you might read one of the corresponding meditations in this book.) Then we pray the Our Father.

5. We pray one Hail Mary on each of the next ten beads. Then we pray the Glory Be on the same small bead as the last Hail Mary.

6. We announce the second decade on the next large bead, reflect, pray the Our Father, then ten Hail Marys, and continue the same pattern for all five decades of the Rosary.

7. We reach the end of the Rosary with the final Glory Be. On the medal that connects the beads, we pray the Hail Holy Queen.

8. Please follow your local custom for other prayers at this point.

9. Make the sign of the cross.

METHOD 2

Meditating with the Rosary throughout the day.

The Rosary tells the story of Jesus, how He came to be born, how He lived, how He died, and how He rose. It helps us call to mind the relationship Jesus had with His Mother Mary. We picture these events or "mysteries," which occurred in the life of Jesus and spend time placing ourselves in the picture we imagine. This helps us connect with the action of God in the event and in our lives today.

In the first Joyful Mystery an angel announces to Mary that God is with her and has a very special role for her to play. She is asked to accept and she says "yes." We imagine what it was like for this teenage girl to say yes to becoming the Mother of Jesus. We then focus our attention on the ways God is calling us to say yes. We ask for Mary's help as we recite the ten Hail Marys.

28

During the day as we travel to work or school or go about our morning tasks, we continue to meditate as we remember Mary's trip to visit her cousin Elizabeth. We reflect on the way Mary and Elizabeth experienced God's presence during this visit. We then focus on the many ways God visits us during the day. We ask Mary to help us recognize God in all we do as we pray the ten Hail Marys.

We continue this process with all five events in the Joyful Mysteries. By the end of the day we have reached the last decade of the Joyful Mysteries. We reflect on the joy and confusion felt by Mary and Joseph in the temple where they found Jesus.

Where did you find Jesus today? Was it in a poor person on the street, an elderly neighbor, a friend, a child, or your husband or wife? The same form of meditation or reflection can accompany you through all four sets of mysteries of the Rosary. Praying this way throughout the day helps us keep God as the center of our lives. It helps prayer become more than a moment or two with God—it becomes a way of life.

THE PRAYERS OF THE ROSARY

When praying the Rosary in groups, one person commonly leads while the other(s) respond. This strengthens the experience of communal prayer.

The Apostles' Creed: The creed is said while holding the crucifix. It is a simple statement of our most fundamental beliefs.

Leader: I believe in God, the Father Almighty, Creator of heaven and earth;
and in Jesus Christ his only Son, our Lord;
who was conceived by the Holy Spirit, born of the Virgin Mary, suffered under Pontius Pilate,

was crucified, dead, and buried. He descended to the dead.
The third day he rose again from the dead. He ascended into heaven
and is seated at the right hand of the Father from where he shall come to judge the living and the dead.

All: I believe in the Holy Spirit, the holy Catholic Church,
the communion of saints, the forgiveness of sins, the resurrection
of the body, and life everlasting. Amen.

Our Father: The large single beads are used to pray the Our Father, the prayer that Jesus taught His disciples when they asked Him how to pray.

Leader: Our Father who is in heaven, holy be your name. Your kingdom come; your will be done on earth as it is in heaven.

All: Give us this day our daily bread, and forgive us our trespasses,
as we forgive those who trespass against us,
and lead us not into temptation, but deliver us from evil.
Amen.

Hail Mary: The smaller beads are used to count the Hail Marys—the prayer that recounts the angel's greeting and what Elizabeth had said to Mary while she was pregnant with Jesus.

Leader: Hail Mary, full of grace, the Lord is with you. Blessed are you among women and blessed is the fruit of your womb, Jesus.

All: Holy Mary, Mother of God, pray for us sinners, now and at the hour of our death. Amen.

Doxology or Glory Be: It is common to pray the doxology after each decade or set of ten Hail Marys. This prayer has its roots in an ancient Jewish prayer, acknowledging God's greatness. But as a Christian prayer it praises the three persons of the Blessed Trinity.

Leader: Glory be to the Father, and to the Son, and to the Holy Spirit.

All: As it was in the beginning, is now, and ever shall be, world without end. Amen.

Hail Holy Queen: The medal which connects the beads is used by some to say the first Our Father and the Hail Holy Queen or *Salve Regina* at the end of the Rosary. This hymn was widely used in church services during the Middle Ages. By the seventeenth century it was part of the Rosary although little is known of how that came to be.

Leader: Hail Holy Queen,

All: Mother of Mercy, our life, our sweetness, and our hope! To you do we cry poor banished children of Eve;
to you do we send up our sighs, mourning and weeping in this valley of tears.

31

Turn then, O most gracious advocate, your eyes of mercy toward us;
and after this our exile, show unto us the blessed fruit of your womb, Jesus.
O clement! O loving! O sweet Virgin Mary!

Prayer to Conclude the Rosary:

Leader: Pray for us, O Holy Mother of God:

All: That we may be made worthy of the promises of Christ.

4

Meditations for Caregivers

by Maggie Hume

Caregivers of Alzheimer's patients need to find some way to become spiritually energized, renewed, and connected with their God. These meditations on the Mysteries of the Rosary written by Maggie Hume come from her many years of caring for her mother who suffered with Alzheimer's. Each relates some piece of everyday life to one of the twenty Mysteries. Alzheimer's patients often revert back to their childhood when in crisis, dealing with each other, or relating to God, bringing profound challenges to those who love and care for them. May these meditations and prayers bring consolation and comfort to all you who are caregivers.

As you say the prayer at the end of each meditation, simply add your own loved one's name in the blank space.

THE JOYFUL MYSTERIES

The First Joyful Mystery: The Annunciation

When the doctor phoned to tell me that she thought Mom had "some type of senile dementia," I was devastated. A battery of tests had found no other cause for my mother's increasingly odd behavior and speech problems. I had been so sure that her problems stemmed from a visit to a new doctor and an increase in her thyroid medication, but I was wrong.

Almost four years ago Mom and Dad moved in with my husband, children, and me so that I could help Dad, whose health is frail, take care of Mom. For years she took care of everyone, now it was our turn. It is now seven years since that initial diagnosis and Mom is in the last weeks of her battle with Alzheimer's disease. Dad and I are in our final weeks as caregivers. It has been quite a journey.

Prayer

I don't know about you Mary, but many times I've questioned my "Yes." So many times it just seems too hard. But then there's a look, or a smile, or an entire good day with _____ and I know my "Yes" was the right decision. Lord, please help me live my "Yes" on the bad days.

The Second Joyful Mystery: The Visitation

The first month that Mom and Dad were living with us was a nightmare. They had barely moved in when Dad had a heart attack and needed open-heart surgery. Dad's hospitalization made Mom's Alzheimer's worse. Or, at least it made my coping skills worse. Dad spent about three weeks in the hospital and then another two weeks in rehab. Then there were months of slow recovery at home.

Mom was completely confused by Dad's absence. She didn't know where he was or why he was gone. Everyday we would visit him in the hospital. She appeared completely unaware of how sick he was. She would ask me the same questions hundreds of times a day: "When is he coming home?" and "Is he coming home now?"

I thought I was going to go nuts, but then a small miracle happened. I ran into a neighbor who told me about a local adult day care program that her mother attended and enjoyed. I took down the number and gave them a call.

Prayer

Mary, you understood what Elizabeth was going through and reached out to her. Help me be aware of the needs of others. Help me appreciate all the many friends I have who have reached out to me.

The Third Joyful Mystery: The Birth of Our Lord

One night soon after Mom had come to live with us I was in the kitchen fixing dinner. When the food was almost ready, my four-year-old son Peter came into the kitchen and started to race his matchbox trucks across the floor.

"Come on Peter, put down the trucks and help me set the table for dinner."

"Okay, Mom," he said and we got out the silverware and napkins.

As we were setting the table, Mom came into the room.

"Maggie, why does HE get to help you set the table? I wanted to do that."

Peter and I looked at each other in mutual disbelief at what we were hearing. I couldn't believe that my mother was whining at me like a petulant child. Peter very reasonably let Grandma set the table and went back to his trucks.

After dinner Peter and I had the first of many talks about Grandma and Alzheimer's disease. I realized that just as I had prepared the older children when a new baby was coming home, I should have prepared Peter for Grandma's arrival. The only problem was that I didn't know what to expect myself.

Prayer

Lord Jesus, my world is fairly chaotic right now. Please bring me your peace. Be born in my heart every day and let your love fill me with joy.

The Fourth Joyful Mystery:
The Presentation in the Temple

The people at our church are just wonderful. No one has ever said not to bring Mom or that her presence at church made anyone uncomfortable. And that's a good thing because Mom loved going to church. Sunday Mass has been an important part of Mom's life since childhood. Whenever she could, she would go during the week too. When she moved in with us, I took her to daily Mass.

We live near the church and pass it in the car many times a day on our way to the supermarket, library, or school. Even when Mom couldn't read very well anymore, she could make out the word "church" and order me to "turn in here now!" Even on days when Mom was very restless and agitated, she was calm in church. She loved the singing and loved the people. She was happy.

Mom is confined to bed now. She can't walk and most of the time she is completely silent. But every day I take her hand in mine and we pray. They are my words, but our prayers.

Prayer

Lord Jesus, your parents presented you to the Father when you were a tiny baby. They recognized your holiness. Help me to recognize the holiness that is within us all.

The Fifth Joyful Mystery:
The Finding of the Child Jesus in the Temple

We were lucky. There never was a problem with Mom wandering out of the house. Maybe our daily walks helped. However, she was very, very restless in the house. This was particularly true at mealtimes.

Every day Mom would wake up very early and want breakfast. Dad would pretend he was asleep until about 5:30 a.m. and then they would eat. On most days we would go to 9:00 a.m. Mass, but, if not, Mom would be ready for lunch about 9:00 a.m. She would fuss and try to "fix lunch" until she actually had lunch at 11:00 a.m. After a brief nap, she would have her walk and then want to "fix dinner" at 1:00 p.m. She would take out knives, forks, plates, glasses, and anything else she found in the cupboard. It wasn't that she was hungry. We gave her plenty of snacks. She just wanted her old job back.

Mom had raised seven children and was the solo chef in the kitchen. We children were not allowed in! At first she helped me prepare meals, but gradually even the simplest task became too hard. And then our all-day mealtimes began.

Prayer

Mary and Joseph were frantic when they couldn't find Jesus as they traveled from Jerusalem. Lord, certain times with _____ make me frantic too. Help me realize that (s)he's just trying to remember what (s)he's supposed to do, but just can't remember.

THE LUMINOUS MYSTERIES

The First Luminous Mystery: The Baptism in the Jordan

Very early in my days as Mom's caregiver I realized that the only way I could cope with the increased stress in my life was through prayer and exercise. Since I need exercise every day, despite sun, rain, or blizzard, we bought a treadmill.

Solving the exercise dilemma proved to be much easier than maintaining daily prayer in my life. Many days were so crazy that "God help us" was the extent of my prayer. The exercising was helping to keep me calm, but I wanted the peace that only prayer can bring. A priest friend suggested that I keep a journal—nothing fancy, just a few lines at the end of the day. So I decided to give it a try. At first, I poured out as much of the day's frustrations as I could in those few lines. Then, gradually, I used the journal to help me focus and pray.

Prayer

Lord, sometimes it is so difficult to recognize you. When you went to John to be baptized, he immediately felt the power of your love. He saw your holiness. Lord, help me to see you in the events of every day so that I too can be immersed in your love.

The Second Luminous Mystery: The Wedding Feast at Cana

One night after dinner I got a phone call from Sister Joan. Sister Joan worked at the adult day care program that Mom attended. "Maggie, I was visiting at the day care center this morning and saw Anne. I'm calling to tell you that I think it is time for her to go to a nursing home. She must be too much for you to manage now." I thanked Sister Joan for her concern and then went to find my husband Kevin to see what he thought of the call.

Kevin said that Sister Joan was right about Mom being too much for one person to handle. However, with Dad, Kevin, and the children I was hardly taking care of Mom alone. We were all in this together! We decided on a "one day at a time" approach. So far we were managing okay. If things got to be more than we could deal with, then we'd consider other care options.

Prayer

At the wedding feast Mary told the waiters "Do whatever he tells you." Mary, help me listen. Help me hear your words of inspiration and peace. Help me to know what's best for _____ and for us.

The Third Luminous Mystery:
The Announcement of the Kingdom

One of the phrases that Mom repeats over and over, hundreds of times a day is "Please forgive me." Sometimes she says it while taking all the items out of a drawer or cupboard. But usually she just repeats the phrase while sitting in her chair. It is amazing how annoying it is for someone to ask for forgiveness over and over, every day.

Just when I thought I couldn't stand to hear that phrase one more time, something changed. I'm not quite sure how it happened but for some reason Mom's repetitive phrases just didn't get to me anymore.

Prayer

Lord, when you announced the Good News you asked your followers to open their hearts and change their ways. I know that it is hard for me to change my actions. _____ can't help repeating what she says, but with your help I can change how I react to her. Thank you Lord for helping me.

The Fourth Luminous Mystery: The Transfiguration

Late afternoons are difficult. That's the time of day when Mom is most agitated and usually I am busy fixing dinner, helping with homework, or running a last minute errand. So it is up to Dad to help settle Mom down. He first tried to get her to watch television with him, but that didn't work because she can't follow the shows anymore. He got frustrated and would yell at her, but she just laughed because she didn't understand what he was saying. Then he tried the Rosary, which he calls "The Prayer."

Now in the late afternoon Dad says, "Come on, Anne, it is time to say The Prayer." He gets out his beads and hands her the Rosary booklet so she can look at the pictures. She is happy. There is peace.

Prayer

Jesus, as you prayed on the hillside the transforming power of God's love shone through you. Help me to experience the transforming power of prayer in my life.

The Fifth Luminous Mystery: The Institution of the Eucharist

My brother Tom recently gave me a photo that was taken at a family reunion at my brother Peter's house. In the photo are my five brothers, my sister, and me, with all our children and spouses, about thirty of us. My parents are seated in the middle of it all. Dad is smiling and happy to be there. Mom looks terrified. The reunion was too much for her to deal with. She didn't know who anyone was and she couldn't wait to go home. Dad and I never left her alone but it didn't do any good. In such a big group, her children and grandchildren were just terrifying strangers.

At first I hated the photo which captures Mom's terror so graphically. Now I'm not so sure. I'm starting to see the entire picture: Mom and Dad are surrounded by a family that loves them very much. Mom's world is very scary for her right now. It is good that we all have a photo to remind us how much she needs to be surrounded by our love.

Prayer

Lord, thank you for the unconditional love that you share in the eucharist with my family and me. Please help me to share this love with _____. Please help me to bring her your peace.

THE SORROWFUL MYSTERIES

The First Sorrowful Mystery: The Agony in the Garden

Without a doubt, being Mom's primary caregiver has been stressful and sometimes overwhelming. But then every so often something happens to remind me that it's not just about me.

For four months now Mom has been confined to bed. She has forgotten just about everything. She must be fed, bathed, changed. She can no longer walk or even sit up. And she hasn't said a word in months, until last week. On Saturday, after I had given her breakfast and bathed her, she turned to me and said, "Please help me." I started to cry. Mom had been silent for so long. She didn't say anything else that day, but I became a little more vigilant. I began expecting her to speak. And I began to wonder more about her agony than my own.

Prayer

Lord, I am not proud to admit this, but I'm sure that if you'd asked me to keep you company during your agony, I would have fallen asleep. Peter, James, and John lived with you and knew you so well, yet they slept through your agony. Lord, I'd like to stay awake and be present for _____ during this time of his/her agony. Please help me.

The Second Sorrowful Mystery:
The Scourging at the Pillar

Mom did not like going to her adult day care program. The facility was wonderful and the staff was terrific, but Mom wanted to stay home. We worked out a compromise. On Mondays and Wednesdays I'd take her to Mass and then to day care. It was a chance for her to get out and socialize and for me to catch my breath and do some errands. Things did not go smoothly.

Mom never recognized the day care building from the outside, but once inside the door her pleading would begin: "I will NOT stay here. Maggie, please take me home. I feel sick." The staff assured me that she was quiet and fine soon after I left, but many times I left in tears. My feelings of guilt were overpowering. I realized that Mom's behavior at home was too difficult for me to manage without a break. Still, I felt so selfish.

Prayer

Sometimes my feelings of guilt and inadequacy are so strong that they completely overwhelm me. They beat me down. Lord, give me your strength. Remind me that I am not alone.

The Third Sorrowful Mystery: The Crowning with Thorns

Once someone actually said to me, "Anne is not your mother anymore. Your mother is gone. This person couldn't possibly be your mother. Your mother would never act like that." The words were meant to be words of comfort—a rationalization of bizarre behavior. But those words were untrue. Anne is my mother, right now and always.

Sometimes Mom's behavior was maddening and inexplicable. And sometimes her behavior was gentle and sweet. More and more now when I look into her eyes there is a blank and vacant stare. Although Alzheimer's disease has altered Mom's behavior, she is still the same person. The other day when I was changing her position in bed, Mom grabbed my hand and said, "This is scary." All I could say was, "Oh, Mom, it's so scary for me too." She's still my Mom.

Prayer

Jesus, when the soldiers placed the crown of thorns on your head they mocked your kingship. They did not understand. Please help me honor and respect _____, especially when she behaves in ways I do not understand.

The Fourth Sorrowful Mystery: The Carrying of the Cross

One of the chores that I had to assume when Mom and Dad moved in was managing their finances. Mom was the money manager in the family. She kept detailed records and organized files. However, by the time I took over their files they were pretty much in shambles. Her check register didn't make any sense at all. Bills were not paid. And every piece of junk mail for the past year was saved and filed.

Mom was absolutely furious with me. Within the few short weeks she had lived with us I had taken away her car keys (doctor's orders) and now I was taking away control of her money. For months Mom told me that she hated me and that she wanted to run away. It was just awful. But very gradually things got better. The constant pleading to be taken to the bank became an occasional question. Then money matters were completely forgotten.

Prayer

Lord, dementia is a very great cross to carry for
_____ and for us. Please help us keep going. Show me how to help without getting crushed.

The Fifth Sorrowful Mystery: The Crucifixion

Hospice comes to our house every day now. Joan, Mom's home health aide, bathes Mom, massages lotion into her very dry skin, and then lavishly splashes her with perfume. It is her daily anointing.

This is not the scary, awful time I thought it would be; it is a peaceful time. Mom cannot move and rarely speaks but she smiles and seems very comfortable. Dad feeds her the liquid meals that are all she can manage now. Her eyes lock on his and she smiles. The days of frantic chaos are over. We play tapes and CDs of familiar church hymns. We hold her hands. We pray.

Every so often I am overcome with the fact of my mother's impending death and I cry and cry. I will miss her so much. Right now I am learning a lot from her about death, just as she's taught me so much about life.

Prayer

Mary, you witnessed the cruel death of your son. Please be with me during the hours of _____ death.

The Glorious Mysteries

The First Glorious Mystery: The Resurrection

About a year ago Mom started calling me "mother." It happened gradually. Usually she would wander into the family room and ask one of the children, "Where is your mother?" Most times I would be sitting right next to the child she had asked. Sometimes, I would be the only person in the room and she'd ask me the question. Once she found me she would begin her inquiry with "Mother...." as in, "Mother, when are we going to eat dinner?" So I became "mother" to my mother.

I have to admit that I loved it when Mom called me "mother." It made me happy that she felt safe, protected, and cared for. About a month before Mom became totally bedridden she collapsed at the hairdresser and was taken to the hospital. Nothing new was discovered but they kept her there for a few days "just in case."

Dad and I went to visit her twice a day and the hospital hired sitters to be with her round the clock. The highlight of each day was the greeting I would get when I walked in the door of Mom's hospital room, "Oh, here's my mother." And a smile would light up her face.

Prayer

Sometimes I wonder how I ever made it through those first years as _____ caregiver. Then I remember that it was you Lord. Thank you.

The Second Glorious Mystery: The Ascension of Our Lord

Every afternoon Mom liked to take a walk. We live in a quiet neighborhood with very little traffic so at first it was okay for her to walk alone. Soon, however, I began to worry that she might get lost so one of our older children or I would accompany her. On more than one of these excursions I was given a geographical theology lesson.

"Maggie, I love walking outside because I love looking at the sky. You know, that's where God lives. When I'm out here I know that God can see me." She was a highly educated woman who might have had another slant on where God lives in her younger days. But the time for theology discussions had passed. I realized that Mom loved her walks so much because that was when she knew God was with her.

Prayer

Lord, I know that you are with me now and always but sometimes I get busy and distracted and forget you are there. Mary, please lead me into the healing presence of your son.

The Third Glorious Mystery: The Descent of the Holy Spirit

The room that Mom and Dad used as a bedroom had been our living room. It is a large room that we had fitted with doors for privacy. One door opens to the front hall and the second door opens to the kitchen. When Mom became confined to bed we placed her hospital bed opposite the door to the kitchen. Propped up in bed with the door open, Mom could see and hear all that was going on in the kitchen and in the family room beyond.

In the afternoons, our two youngest children, Peter and Maura, would come home from school and shout a "Hi, Grandma" in Mom's direction. At mealtimes the door was left open so Mom could be present with us at the kitchen table. The whole time she was in bed she was still right in the middle of our family life. After the years of chaos, it was a very peaceful and healing time.

Prayer

Dear God, thank you for the many gifts you have given me—especially my family. They have accepted _____ illness and encouraged me to carry on when I felt too exhausted to continue. I couldn't have done it without them.

The Fourth Glorious Mystery:
The Assumption of Our Lady into Heaven

Mom died on the fourth of July. It was one of the most beautiful and peaceful events in my life. A few days before her death, her breathing changed and she had difficulty swallowing, so Hospice started her on morphine and told us that the end was near. My sister came to help and other relatives who hadn't visited Mom recently came to say good-bye. On the morning of Mom's death, her youngest brother came to visit. He knelt by Mom's bed and prayed. Then he, Dad, and I stood around her and visited for about an hour. When it was time for him to leave I walked my uncle to his car. He said to me, "Maggie, tell your mother it's time for her to go now." And that's what I did.

Back in the house my husband, father, and I gathered around Mom's bed and we prayed. Then I told Mom that it was time for her to go to heaven and named everyone we loved who had died that she'd see when she got to heaven. When I was finished, Mom sighed, and was gone.

Prayer

Thank you God for the wonderful gift of family and friends and the love we share. Although we will be heartbroken at the hour of death, we will rejoice knowing that _____ is with you.

The Fifth Glorious Mystery: The Coronation of the Blessed Virgin Mary

Two weeks after Mom died we went on vacation to Cape Cod. One rainy day when I was browsing in a wonderful shop, I saw a jewelry display that was quite attractive. "Wouldn't Mom love to have that pin," I thought. And then I remembered that Mom had died. Tears started coming and I made a quick exit out of the store. The rain had stopped and I found a dry bench under a big tree. Sitting there I realized that something wonderful had just happened.

In the store I was thinking of Mom as I had known her before her illness. Those memories had been buried under the day-to-day realities of caregiving. Now all the wonderful memories came flooding in.

Prayer

Lord, _____ and I have always been so close. We've had so many wonderful times together. Thank you for helping me rejoice in the memories.

$$\underline{5}$$

Meditations for Loved Ones and Patients Together

by Beth Mahoney

The following meditations on the Mysteries of the Rosary are written for those who are caring for patients in a nursing home, hospital, or private home, perhaps to be used when praying with someone who has Alzheimer's. Since the prayers of the Rosary are some of those we learn first in life, they can be a tremendous comfort to those with Alzheimer's and to you who care for them. The Rosary is rhythmic and repetitive, often bringing calm and tender moments of shared prayer.

THE JOYFUL MYSTERIES

1. The Annunciation

The angel Gabriel was sent by God to ask Mary to be the Mother of his Son. Mary was frightened for she did not know the angel or how this could be. Mary took time to think about it and said, "Yes" with all of her faith in the God that she knew and trusted.

There are times when we are asked to do things that frighten us and we are not always ready to do them. We pray that like Mary we may say yes to what we are asked to do and that we trust in God. We pray for the grace of perseverance and of giving over our lives to God's tender care and holy design.

Pray the first decade

2. The Visitation

Mary went to visit her cousin, Elizabeth, to help her during her time of need. The two greeted each other and felt the presence of God between them. This gave both of them great joy.

There are times when we visit with those we have not seen in a long time. Sometimes we do not remember them or recognize the person we once knew. May we experience Mary's joy as we reach out to the presence of God within those we greet. We pray for the grace of acceptance.

Pray the second decade.

3. The Birth of our Lord

Mary and Joseph traveled many miles to find a home where Mary could give birth to her son. They found a simple place in a stable and they wrapped him in swaddling clothes and laid him in the manger.

May we hold a place in our hearts for Jesus that is simple. May people recognize him in us. We pray for the grace of love.

Pray the third decade.

4. The Presentation in the Temple

As Mary and Joseph brought Jesus as an infant to the temple to present him to the Lord in accordance with the law, Mary heard the words of Simeon and Ana, and kept all this in her heart. She was told that the hearts of many would be pierced because of her son.

Each time we pray for someone, we bring him or her to the Lord. May our loved ones know of the presence of God in their lives. We pray for the grace of communication.

Pray the fourth decade.

5. The Finding of the Child Jesus in the Temple

When Jesus was a child, Mary and Joseph brought him to the temple and became separated from him. Jesus was lost for three days and when Mary found him he was among the leaders in the temple listening to them and asking them questions.

When we have family members that are lost or feel lost ourselves, may they be found in the presence of God listening to him and asking him questions. We pray for the grace of determination.

Pray the fifth decade.

THE LUMINOUS MYSTERIES

1. The Baptism in the Jordan

Jesus was baptized in the Jordan by John to begin his public ministry. The sky opened and a voice from the heavens proclaimed, "This is my beloved Son, in whom I am well pleased."

May we listen to the words of Jesus and grow in our love for him. Let us pray for the grace of wisdom so that we understand that God is pleased with us just as we are.

Pray the first decade.

2. The Wedding Feast at Cana

Mary said to the server, "Do whatever he tells you." Jesus changed water into wine and preformed his first public miracle.

May we do what Jesus tells us to do and grow to trust in his words to us. Let us pray for the grace of knowledge.

Pray the second decade.

3. The Proclamation of the Kingdom

Jesus gave witness to the importance of healing, forgiveness, and reconciliation in life. Throughout his public ministry, he constantly invited people to change their ways and follow him.

May we have a conversion of heart and experience the healing and forgiving presence of Jesus in the sacrament of reconciliation. May we let go of our grudges. Let us pray for the grace of forgiveness and reconciliation.

Pray the third decade.

4. The Transfiguration

Jesus took Peter, James, and John and went up the mountain to pray. While praying he changed in appearance and they wanted to stay on the mountain with him.

We see God in a different light each time we pray for our lives to change. Let us pray for the grace of conversion.

Pray the fourth decade.

5. The Institution of the Eucharist

Jesus teaches us about serving those in need when he washes the feet of his disciples. Afterwards he said them, "What I have just done for you, now you must go and do for others."

May we have the courage to serve others with this same humility that Jesus showed at the Last Supper. And may we graciously accept the service of others when we need help. Let us pray for the grace of courage.

Pray the fifth decade.

THE SORROWFUL MYSTERIES

1. The Agony in the Garden

The night before he died, Jesus went alone into the garden to pray. He asked his Father if what he was about to live could pass him by. He prayed that if not, God's will would be done.

When we feel alone and go to God in prayer, may we trust in God's will for us and live what God asks of us with strength and courage. Let us pray for the grace to go to God when we need help.

Pray the first decade.

2. The Scourging at the Pillar

Jesus was beaten while his hands were tied to a pole and soldiers whipped him. He endured this needless suffering for he was an innocent man free of sin.

There are times in our lives that we suffer needlessly because of misunderstandings or the ignorance of others regarding what we are and how we are feeling. Let us pray for the grace of perseverance.

Pray the second decade.

3. The Crowning with Thorns

The soldiers placed a crown of thorns on the head of Jesus, placed a reed in his hand and a purple robe over his body and mocked him.

There are times in life when we find ourselves being mocked because of who we are or what we do or don't do. We don't always understand why this happens. Let us pray for the grace of endurance.

Pray the third decade.

4. The Carrying of the Cross

Jesus fell several times trying to carry his cross to Calvary. Simon of Cyrene helped him.

As we struggle to carry our crosses, may we get up after we fall and accept the assistance of those around us who will offer to help us. Let us pray for the grace of humility.

Pray the fourth decade.

5. The Crucifixion

Jesus died on the cross to shatter the power of sin and to give us eternal life. Such is the power of love.

When we are faced with our own death may we be ready to pray like Jesus did, "Into your hands I commend my spirit." Let us pray for the grace of surrender.

Pray the fifth decade.

THE GLORIOUS MYSTERIES

1. The Resurrection

Jesus rose from the dead after being in the tomb for three days. On the road to Emmaus they recognized him in the breaking of the bread.

As we look for Jesus may we always recognize him in the breaking of the bread. Let us pray for the grace to see the Risen Lord in our lives.

Pray the first decade.

2. The Ascension of our Lord

Jesus ascended into heaven before his disciples. He said, "I must go and see my Father and send the Holy Spirit, the Paraclete, to be with you."

Jesus left the disciples to ascend to Heaven. May we never believe that Jesus is absent from our lives. Let us pray for the grace of believing.

Pray the second decade.

3. The Descent of the Holy Spirit

The disciples were gathered in the upper room when the Spirit came like tongues of fire and rested on the head of each person.

May we be open to receive the Holy Spirit into our lives, as did the followers of Jesus on the day of Pentecost. Let us pray for the gifts of the Spirit.

Pray the third decade.

4. The Assumption of our Lady into Heaven

Mary was assumed into heaven body and soul. She lived her life in faithfulness to God and gave witness to a life of trust.

With Mary as our model, may we live our "Yes" in trust and faithfulness to all that God asks of us. Let us pray for the grace of trusting in God.

Pray the fourth decade.

5. The Coronation of the Blessed Virgin Mary

Mary was crowned "Queen of Heaven and Earth." As holy model of discipleship and our intercessor, Mary reminds us that our prayers are heard and answered.

May we go to Mary, trusting in her intercession for us, as we place our intentions before her son, our Lord, Jesus Christ. Let us pray for the grace of piety.

Pray the fifth decade.

References and Resources

REFERENCES

John of the Cross, Saint. *Dark Night of the Soul*. Garden City, New York: Image Books, 1959.

Klein, Melanie. *Envy and Gratitude and Other Works*. New York: Delacorte Press, 1975.

Ulanov, Ann and Barry. *Religion and the Unconscious*. Philadelphia: The Westminster Press, 1975.

Ulanov, Ann and Barry. *Primary Speech: A Psychology of Prayer*. Atlanta: John Knox Press, 1982.

RESOURCES

Administration on Aging
Washington, DC
1-202-619-0724
www.aoa.gov

Alzheimer's Association
Chicago
1-800-272-3900
www.alz.org

Alzheimer's Disease Education and Referral Center (ADEAR)
Silver Spring
1-800-438-4380
www.alzheimers.org

Alzheimer's Disease International
London
011-44-207-620-3011
www.Alz.co.uk

Alzheimer's Foundation of America (AFA)
New York
1-866-AFA-8484
www.alzfdn.org

**Alzheimer's Women's Association for Research and
Education (A.W.A.R.E.)**
Dallas
1-800-515-8201
www.alzdallas.org

American Society on Aging
San Francisco
1-415-974-9600
www.asaging.org

Eldersearch
New York, NY
1-800-259-4636
www.eldersearch.com

Family Caregiver Alliance
San Francisco
445-434-3388 in CA
800-445-8106
www.caregiver.org

National Association on Aging
Bethesda, MD
1-301-496-1752
www.nia.nih.gov

Acknowledgments

I wish to thank Fr. John J. Malecki, a psychologist and priest in the diocese of Albany, New York, for offering a portion of his dissertation to this book. Fr. Malecki has provided pastoral care to patients suffering from Alzheimer's disease for many years. Likewise, I offer much gratitude to Maggie Hume, from Clifton Park, New York, who wrote the reflections for the twenty Mysteries of the Rosary from her own lived experience of taking care of her mother. I thank Laetitia Rhatigan and the members of the Mission Advisory Council from Albany, New York, for initiating this project.

More than a year ago, I met with then Publisher Frank Cunningham, and Mary Andrews, Director of Marketing at Ave Maria Press, to discuss writing a book for family members and caregivers of Alzheimer's patients. We wanted them to understand how they can pray with their loved ones, even in the advanced years of this painful and often frightening disease. Frank Cunningham passed this opportunity on to Bob Hamma, Editorial Director, who turned the manuscript over to Eileen Ponder. I am especially grateful to Eileen for all of her guidance, encouragement, and support in the editing process of this book.

In a very special way, I am most grateful to Father John Phalen, CSC, president of Holy Cross Family Ministries for giving me the responsibility of this project. I am grateful to him for sharing his personal family experience about his dad in writing the foreword. His undying support, belief in this book, and his confidence in me to complete the project has certainly been a tremendous gift to me.

Lastly, it was with the inspiration of Mary, our Blessed Mother, and Servant of God Father Patrick Peyton, CSC, that I was able to pull this book together and focus on the content and objective of working on this project. Perhaps this is the confirmation I needed that Mary can give a caregiver the wisdom and calm necessary to help an Alzheimer's patient deal with their fragmented experiences. I am very grateful for the many hours spent in prayer asking for the guidance of Servant of God Father Patrick Peyton, CSC, in living out his vision that a family that prays together stays together.

Beth Mahoney